SAL

A Tale of Many Feathers!
(Sal is a Laugh a Minute!)

Witnessed by me,
Anna Marie

Copyright: 2013 Anna Marie Petrarca Gire

All Rights Reserved. No part of this book may be reproduced or transmitted in any form or by any means, electronic or mechanical, including photocopying, recording, or by an information storage and retrieval system (except by a reviewer who may quote brief passages in a review to be printed in a magazine, newspaper or on the Internet) without permission in writing from the publisher.

ISBN: 978-1-937958-17-6 hard cover

ISBN: 978-1-937958-18-3 soft cover

ISBN: 978-1-937958-19-0 ebook

LCCN: 2013941351

Red Engine Press (www.redenginepress.com)

Bridgeville, PA

Printed in the United States.

This book is dedicated to

Heidi and Heather Schmidt,

and Dana and Dara Petrarca

the Best of the Best!

There is nothing in which the birds differ more from man than the way in which they can build and yet leave a landscape as it was before.

~ Robert Lynd (1879 - 1949)

Goffins Cockatoo cacatua goffini
Tanimbar Islands Indonesia

There is not much information about cockatoos from the Indonesian Islands or their habitat in the wild. Cockatoos are noisy birds, usually seen in small flocks. These birds typically feed on nuts, berries, fruit, and insects as well as blossoms, feeding in treetops and usually in pairs during the breeding season. As a rule, cockatoos nest in tree hollows and the normal clutch is generally two eggs.

TABLE OF CONTENTS

Chapter 1 - In the Beginning - 1
Chapter 2 - The Merry-Go-Round - 7
Chapter 3 - The Thermostat - 13
Chapter 4 - Pig - 19
Chapter 5 - And Then There Were Two - 23
Chapter 6 - Sal's "Friend" - 29
Chapter 7 - The Dogs - 35
Chapter 8 - The Great Escapes - 45
Chapter 9 - My Mom and Sal - 55
Chapter 10 - Sal Visits a Clip Joint - 63
Chapter 11 - Sal's Christmas Miracle - 67
Chapter 12 - The Miracle Continues - 77
Chapter 13 - Proper Nutrition - 81

Over increasingly large areas of the United States, spring now comes unheralded by the return of the birds, and the early mornings are strangely silent where once they were filled with the beauty of bird song.

~ Rachel Carson, "Silent Spring"

Sal enjoying a cup of tea

Chapter 1
"In the Beginning..."

Salvatore Ricci, otherwise known as Sal, started life free as a bird. But that freedom came to an end around 1978 when Sal was birdnapped, probably from Indonesia or Malaysia, and brought to the United States. Afterward, Sal's trail is hazy, but the story goes that Sal eventually ended up with a veterinary student in Hartford, Connecticut.

"In the Beginning…"

According to that same tale, a woman from Urbana, Illinois, Debbie Nelson and her dog Deuce, went to visit Ms. Nelson's friend — that same veterinary student from Connecticut — and ended up bringing Sal back to Illinois. I imagine the trip was interesting, since Sal and Deuce shared the back seat on that long hot trip. Sal must have been "pacing" back and forth in his cage trying very hard to escape, while Deuce wondered how he got stuck with such a noisy little creature.

Sal is a Goffins Cockatoo — and from wherever he was birdnapped, his trip was probably not comfortable nor something that Sal wanted. But Sal had adjusted to his fate, lucky to find a good home. He made himself very comfortable with Ms. Nelson and Deuce. He snacked on lemons and other fruits and vegetables — and soon settled into a routine.

After a while, Ms. Nelson had to leave town due to a death in her family. And so the search began for a place that would keep Sal for the week that she would be away. Ms. Nelson found a pet store that boarded birds and she left thinking Sal was safe. But during that week, the pet store was burglarized. Along with the other exotic birds, Sal was once again birdnapped. We can only imagine where Sal was — maybe in some dark smoky room, where the thieves who stole him plotted yet more sinister crimes?

SAL

Sal enjoying a snack

"In the Beginning..."

Sal, of course, would be plotting his escape. The thieves were finally captured and Sal, the only remaining bird, was identified through some markings on his little bird body. More than a year later, Sal was returned to Ms. Nelson much better-behaved than the last time she saw him. Apparently, the thieves had a way with birds. Of course, there probably isn't much use for bird training in prison.

Regrettably for them, Sal remained with Ms. Nelson and Deuce for several years — bringing them, I am sure, much joy and happiness. After all, who wouldn't be happy with this little creature that paces and screams all day???

In 1987, March, spring break, my life changed in very odd ways. Ms. Nelson was leaving for a week, and I offered to bird sit, never imagining that Sal would thenceforth be a permanent addition to my life, affording me "a laugh a minute." (Ms. Nelson's words, not mine.) I never really thought about keeping Sal. It just happened.

And so began some of the most amazing stories that I ever thought I would be a part of — stories that are mostly funny — and always interesting.

Trafficking in rare and exotic wildlife is a global business, worth $10-20 billion annually. Birds are among the most popular animals sought after for the exotic pet trade.

www.bornfreeusa.org

To stand at the edge of the sea, to sense the ebb and the flow of the tides, to feel the breath of a mist moving over a great salt marsh, to watch the flight of shore birds that have swept up and down the surf lines of the continents for untold thousands of years, to see the running of the old eels and the young shad to the sea, is to have knowledge of things that are as nearly eternal as any earthly life can be.

~ Rachel Carson, "Silent Spring"

You can't catch me!

Chapter 2

"The Merry go Round"

Life with Sal was challenging. I felt a little sorry for him and thought about letting him stay outside the cage for short periods of time. Once Sal was out, he was out. He flew from window to window and occasionally landed on the ceiling fans, where he never stopped long enough to be captured. Sal even looked happy during his little exercises (whatever a happy look is for a bird) and when I eventually captured him, he always looked a little sad when he had to go back in the cage. And it was necessary for Sal to be back in the cage. In a moment, Sal would bite wires in half, take a chunk out of the plaster with his beak and — finding the head that looked the most interesting — swoop down and perch for a bit. Sal was soon feared and shunned by all within his flight plan. But he was liked by Dave, my husband, who became Sal's non-feathered friend, and me. Dave thought Sal should always be uncaged. I thought so too, but since I got stuck cleaning up after Sal, he went back in the cage after his little excursions.

Sal's personal merry-go-round

The most exciting event of Sal's evening turned out to be the ceiling fan. When Sal landed on it, the fan went round and round — like Sal's own personal merry go round. I was sure that Sal was enjoying that no one could catch him up there. The more we tried, the faster the fan turned. Sal, of course, was propelling it — he had dismantled its power source the first time he landed. So we would spend precious time trying to figure a way to get Sal down and Sal was never ready to get off his fun ride. Exasperated, I would pick up the broom and coax Sal onto the handle. Once this was accomplished, Sal was retired to the cage for the night.

It was always the highest point in the house that interested Sal. I imagine he felt pretty superior up there while we were far below, begging him to come down.

This little activity went on for an embarrassingly long time. Eventually, I tired of the game and made some changes; but that's another story.

"The Merry go Round"

According to the Worldwatch Institute, nearly one-third of the globe's parrot species are threatened with extinction due to pressures from the pet trade and from habitat destruction.

www.bornfreeusa.org

A bird does not sing because it has an answer.
It sings because it has a song.

~ Chinese Proverb

Sal lands on what is left of the thermostat

CHAPTER 3

"THE THERMOSTAT"

"A small device used to regulate the temperature in one's home or business."

For Sal, the thermostat became a wonderland for destruction. Sal loved the thermostat, landing on it whenever the opportunity arose, which it did, often. I was able to catch him right away, and remove his curious little body from the device.

The more we removed Sal from the thermostat, the more attractive it became. Sal would perch on the curtain rod, look longingly at the thermostat, swoop down, and try repeatedly to see if the device could be destroyed in one quick movement. My speedy response usually saved it from certain destruction.

That changed when Dave decided not to put Sal in a safe place when he left the house. One day, I returned home from work and the house was unusually hot. I went to check the thermostat and found most of it scattered on the dining room floor.

Sal was clucking away on his perch in the hall looking very innocent. I attempted to turn the thermostat down, but it wouldn't move. It just sat there while the house became hotter and hotter. The mercury had also been bitten into, so I was sure that Sal had done himself in, but he never suffered any ill effects from the mercury. (Sometimes, Sal seems to truly be a Super Bird.)

I couldn't turn the thermostat down and so for some inexplicable reason, I called his former owner, Debbie, and said quite frantically, because by now I was sure the house might explode from the heat:

"WHAT should I do?"

SAL

She said quite calmly, with a hint of a smile in her voice, "Maybe you should call a plumber." Now why didn't I think of that?

I hung up the phone and realized that it was now about 90 degrees in the house. I called the plumber and a woman answered. In my somewhat controlled voice, I explained the dilemma, "My bird *ate* my thermostat!"

There was dead silence for a moment. Then she repeated what I had said, cheerfully and with a little disbelief — and asked if I wanted someone to come out right away. Hmmm ... right now? Or later, when the house had melted away?

The repairperson came, and he said with a smile, "The bird ate the thermostat!" — and he said it again and again. Funny for him.

Sal was now in big trouble. I tried to watch him closely, but he had Dave on his side. So we continued to play games, me watching Sal, and Sal waiting for that special moment — the moment when I *wasn't* looking. Of course, it happened again! Sal wasn't near the thermostat, but it was not working and Sal had to be the culprit. Who or what else would dismantle the thermostat?

Once again, I called the repair shop and once again talked with the same woman, who with the same bemused voice, said, "So the bird ate the thermostat?"

This was starting to look like a habit, so I asked the repairperson to protect the thermostat with a plastic box. Now Sal had a real surface to land on, but the thermostat was safe.

Or so I thought. Eventually, Sal figured a way to dismantle the box, but the thermostat stayed intact. Sal had better things to do.

Since its passage by Congress in 1992, the Wild Bird Conservation Act has cut poaching rates from between an estimated 20-50%, proving that limits on legal trade can help struggling bird populations.

www.bornfreeusa.org

SAL

Not even Bart Simpson can distract Sal when he is on a mission

Some birds are not meant to be caged, that's all. Their feathers are too bright, their songs too sweet and wild. So you let them go, or when you open the cage to feed them they somehow fly out past you. And the part of you that knows it was wrong to imprison them in the first place rejoices, but still, the place where you live is that much more drab and empty for their departure.

~ Stephen King

Sal's pal

Chapter 4

"Pig"

Sal and Pig have a special relationship. What that relationship is, only Sal knows for sure.

One year for Christmas, Dave received a pig cookie jar as a gift. You know the kind — it makes an "oinking" sound whenever the head is raised.

Sal was intrigued right away with this new addition and flew over to find out what Pig was all about. Sal soon learned that the lid could be lifted up with a well-placed beak under the pig's head. Once that was accomplished, Sal could reach in and grab a beak full of cookies. Some were for Sal and some would be thrown to the floor, much to the delight of the dogs that waited patiently below for the drop. Sal wasn't really fond of the dogs, and the dogs were not very fond of Sal, but this was one thing they all enjoyed.

It wasn't long before Sal and Pig bonded, Sal becoming very fond and possessive of Pig. Whenever anyone went near Pig, even if it was just to wipe off the counter, Sal would fly in, swoop down, and get very close to Pig, making a weird clucking sound and acting aggressively to whoever was near Pig. Getting a cookie out of Pig was almost impossible. Sal wanted everyone away from Pig and was determined to protect this new friend. Such loyalty.

I never really knew what this relationship was between Sal and Pig, but even now, many years later, Sal exhibits the same behavior whenever I go near Pig.

Pig no longer holds cookies, but Pig does hold Sal's heart. They meet regularly on the buffet and do whatever it is that they do, and I really don't want to know any more about that relationship.

SAL

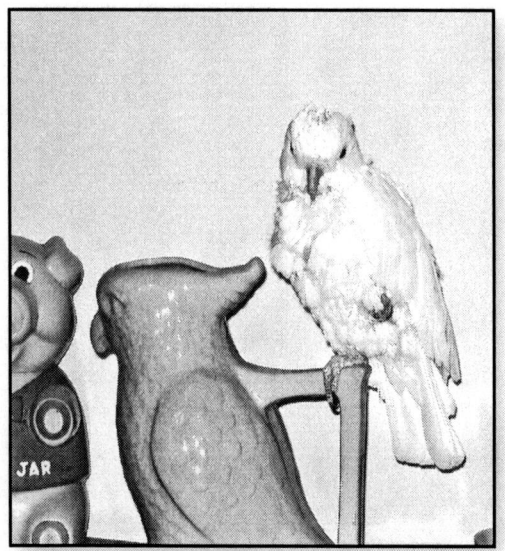

Sal and close friends on the counter

Despite claims about protecting endangered species, most birds in captive breeding programs are produced solely for commercial gain, and are not part of any official conservation program.

www.bornfreeusa.org

God loved the birds and invented trees. Man
loved the birds and invented cages.

~ Jacques Deval

Just try and take my money!

Chapter 5

"And then there were two, Pigs that is"

Sal's obsession with pigs isn't limited to just Pig. One year for our anniversary, I gave Dave a brass piggy bank, nice gift, huh? Sal liked landing on the new Pig, but wasn't aware that money was inside. He liked money, coins especially — he has been known to rip bills to pieces. We learned to put paper money far away from Sal. He could always

"AND THEN THERE WERE TWO, PIGS THAT IS"

Sal's savings account

locate where Dave or I left our change, grab a beak full and fly off to investigate his newfound treasure in private. He would drop the coins, pick them up and then place them in a sort of row, becoming possessive of his coins when anyone attempted to take them away from him. Sal had his little nest egg, so to speak, socked away for his rainy day.

One day, he spied my mom putting money in the bank, and Sal became very excited by this new activity. So we gave him a few pennies and he began the process of placing his money in the

Sal and Other Pig meeting on the windowsill for a chat — or something

"And then there were two, Pigs that is"

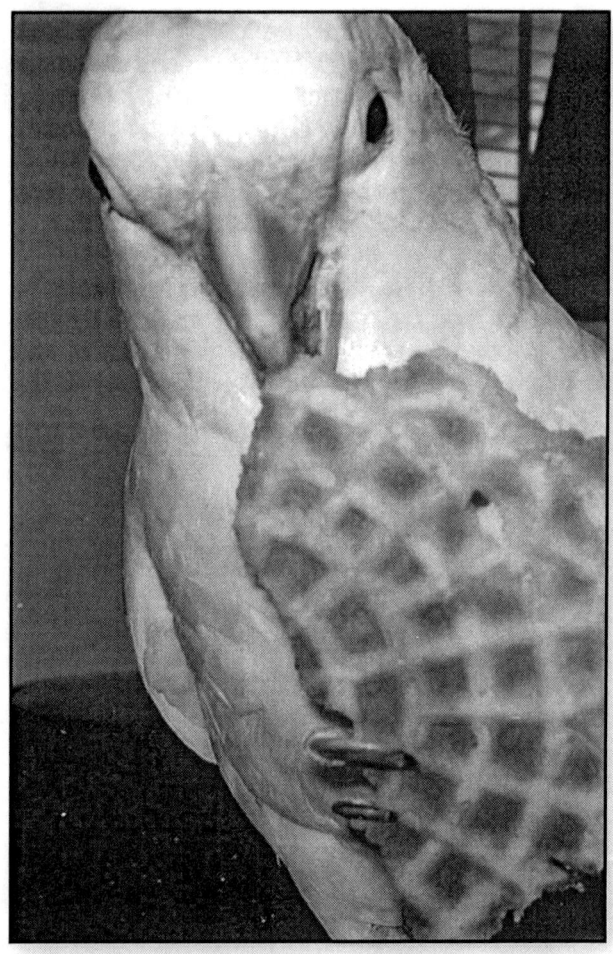

Sal's favorite cookie, a Holiday Pizzelle

slot. Sal was not happy when he couldn't retrieve his coins — and tried for a very long time to pull them out with his little bird feet. Never successful, he became frustrated. Instead of quitting, he looked for more coins to deposit — and stymied, repeated the process for long periods of time. He tired of this after a while, but would occasionally perch on the brass pig and attempt to make a withdrawal. No luck, but it kept him busy for awhile, giving us all a reprieve. Sal needs to be doing something. If it isn't productive or arranged, it is usually destructive and annoying.

Interesting connection, Sal, the cockatoo, Pig the cookie jar, and Other Pig, his own personal bank.

Breeding facilities often resemble nothing more than warehouses. "Breeder" birds are routinely placed with in small cages without any environmental enrichment.

www.bornfreeusa.org

I hope you love birds too. It is economical. It saves going to heaven.

~ Emily Dickinson (1830 - 1886)

Tennis anyone?

CHAPTER 6

"SAL'S FRIEND"

Someone who knew someone who knew me, rescued a Conure — and needed a place for the bird to stay until a permanent home could be located. His name was Pablo, and he was very timid and skittish due to the abuse he experienced in his last home. I agreed to keep him for a short

"Sal's friend"

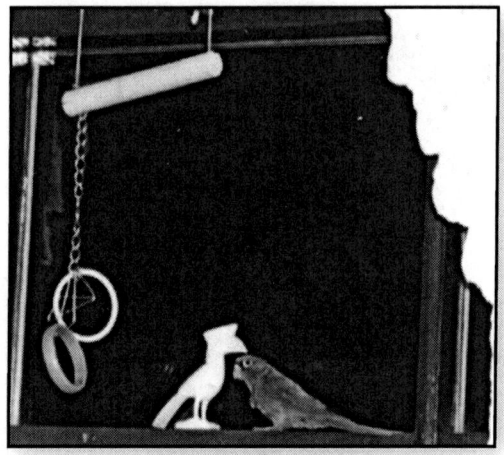

Pablo and friend

period of time, not knowing how Sal would like this new addition.

In fact, Sal didn't like anything about Pablo. Sal would scream and try to attack poor Pablo, and I quickly moved him and Sal to different rooms. However, Sal would look for him in the air and on the floor. Sal was on a mission, peeking in corners, flying to the fans, landing on window sills, craning his little bird neck to see where this new threat to his kingdom had hidden. Pablo was happy in his new room, lots of food and water, things to explore and play with and no mean people or Sal. Pablo did manage to escape from his new room in a mere two days (I am always amazed at a bird's resourcefulness.) Once out, Pablo was even harder to catch than Sal. Small and fast, Pablo would dart from place to place with Sal trying in vain to catch him, but he wasn't quite as fast as Pablo.

Pablo found his way downstairs to the family room where I was finally able to capture him. He seemed to be content going back to his room, where he ate and drank for a long time. We found him a permanent home and Sal was once again in charge of his kingdom.

So many exotic birds end up like Pablo, abused and abandoned. Parrots do not belong inside, but should instead be outside, flying around with lots of fresh air and trees to land on. Remember if you do purchase one of these birds, it's a life commitment since parrots can live 50 years or more. Sal and I have been together for a very long time, 26 years as of March 2013.

"SAL'S FRIEND"

It's their birthright ...

Many people are unprepared to provide lifelong care for birds who, depending on species, can live for between 20 to 70 years. Many birds are neglected, relinquished to overcrowded shelters or sanctuaries, or are abandoned in the wild (where they are likely to perish.)

www.bornfreeusa.org

Much talking is the cause of danger. Silence is the means of avoiding misfortune. The talkative parrot is shut up in a cage. Other birds, without speech, fly freely about.

~ Saskya Pandita

Jumper ponders the question, why is Sal here?????

Chapter 7

"The Dogs"

Sal doesn't like any other animals in our home except Pig, and of course, no one has determined what the allure of Pig is for Sal.

Sal has lived with seven dogs and tried to bully all of them. There was Puppy, Taps, Honnah, Jumper, Sammy the Dog, then Lion — who was only here for a short period before joining the other dogs in dog heaven. Now Sal has Roscoe to annoy.

The only dog that Sal stayed away from was Puppy. Puppy was very attached to me and had no intention of tolerating Sal's obnoxious behavior — and took that stand right away. As for the other dogs, whenever any one of them walked into a room, Sal would swoop down and run right up to them getting as close as possible — and the dogs immediately ran downstairs. Roscoe, like his predecessors, prefers that Sal stay very far away from him.

We could never figure out why Sal has never been hurt by the dogs — must be some kind of super bird luck.

Maybe the dogs tolerated Sal because wherever Sal is, food was sure to drop to the floor. And Sal is always eating — not just bird food, but whatever is available. Sal ate, dropped the dregs — and the dogs were always there to snatch up whatever food fell their way. Roscoe continues the tradition of waiting patiently for the drop and is often rewarded for that patience. The one thing the dogs and Sal like to do together — eat.

Most evenings, Dave and I took the dogs for a walk. Sal wanted to go for that walk with all the dogs, so he would get down on the floor, grab hold of the leash, and get pulled around by the dogs who were acting as if going for a walk was the most wonderful event of a lifetime. Sal, of course, didn't go for the walk. Instead, he sat on the windowsill screaming loud enough to be heard two or three blocks away — and continued screaming until we returned from the walk.

Sal did get the obligatory biscuit when we returned home, just like the dogs did. The dogs sat patiently until Sal dropped the biscuit and some lucky dog received two biscuits that night. The walks continue and Roscoe is often rewarded with two biscuits after our walk.

Every once in a while, the dogs would get a break — Sal would plot and execute "The Escape."

"The Dogs"

Sal trying to figure out, "How does this harness work?"

SAL

Sal looks wistfully out of the window

"The Dogs"

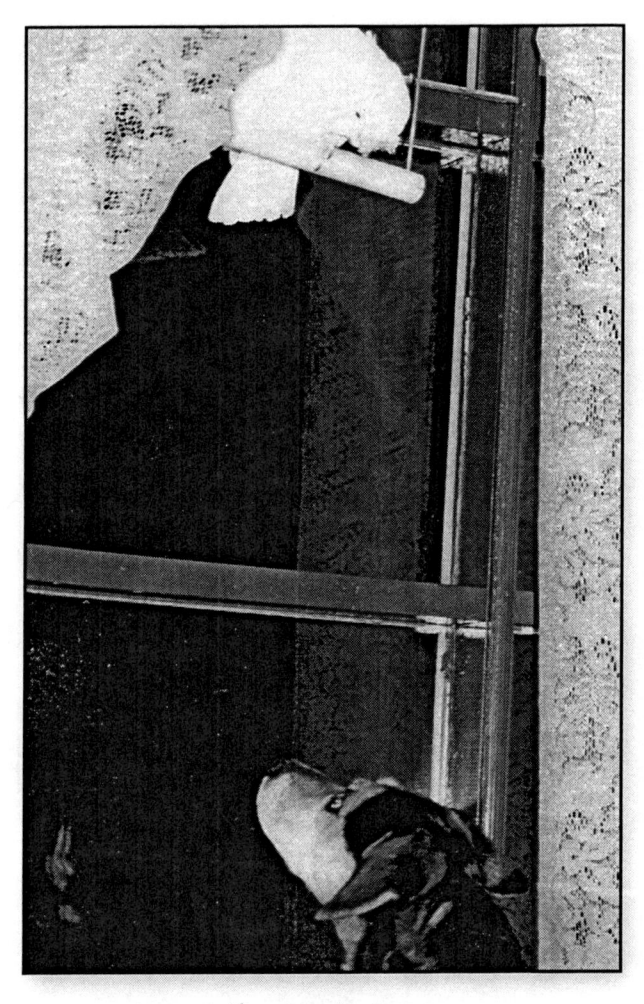

Sal's nemesis, Puppy

SAL

To all the dogs who came before...

"The Dogs"

Scan to see video of Sal & Lion

Replacing the demand for birds as "pets" with a demand for preserving birds in the wild will reduce welfare problems associated with captivity while increasing the support of genuinely effective conservation efforts.

www.bornfreeusa.org

Mockingbirds don't do one thing but make music for us to enjoy. They don't do one thing but sing their hearts out for us. That's why it's a sin to kill a mockingbird.

~ Harper Lee

Honnah and a belligerent Sal

Chapter 8

"The Great Escapes"

Sal's first escape came on a warm summer day. Dave was standing in the doorway, facing the backyard with Sal on his shoulder. The door was open slightly — just enough for a bird to fly though — so Sal did just that. What a wonderful feeling that must have been, flying somewhere other than inside the house! Dave and my brother tried to track Sal down without any luck. I returned home from work and found Dave and my brother riding around on his bike, looking up in the sky. I thought it was kind of odd, but…

Soon I joined in, riding around on my bike, looking up towards the sky and calling out to Sal. Off and on throughout the day, there were sightings of Sal. I had posted flyers around the neighborhood, called the local radio stations, and searched most of the day with Dave and some friends. I contacted the University of Illinois Veterinary Clinic. They advised that Sal might stay within a mile of where we lived. "Find the highest point," they said, "and Sal will probably be there." Night came. Without locating Sal, we stopped searching but resumed first thing the next day, Saturday.

Sal was spotted all around the neighborhood. No human could miss that delightful scream, but we were unable to actually see him.

As the day progressed, the weather turned ominous. The sky darkened and the winds kicked up. A tornado was on the way, and we really wanted to catch Sal before that happened. Around 6 pm, almost 24 hours after the escape, Sal was sighted about two blocks from our home in a very tall tree in the parking lot of a local elementary school. Dave and I went to the school with a ladder — and Dave started to climb the tree. By this time, a crowd had gathered. The winds were fierce and the rain was just starting to fall. What a sight we must have made — me calling the bird and Dave climbing the tree against the wind and the rain.

Finally, Dave did get a hold of Sal — who by this time was frightened — and handed him to me. Still spooked, Sal took a big bite of my finger. I quickly put him in the cage and took him home. Someone advised me to get a tetanus shot because Sal was gone for that 24 hours and could have contracted some exotic avian disease — so I did.

Sal's first big escape ended right before a storm. He was okay, even though he looked a bit sad. After that, I kept a close eye on his whereabouts. Sometimes other folks did not.

One sunny day, when a friend left the door open for a moment to bring in a ladder, Sal saw the opportunity to escape. In a moment, Sal was out the door flying high and quickly out of sight.

And so the search began again. We did the usual — posted the flyers that my friend kindly put together, rode bikes up and down the neighborhood streets, called the radio station — but no luck. But then Sal was sighted in a yard about two blocks from our home. Dave and I went to the yard where we found him high in a tree, alternately eating and throwing apples to the ground below. We started to call, "Sal, Sal, come on down!" He was probably thinking, "Are you crazy, why would I do that?"

"The Great Escapes"

We obviously needed a better plan. We knew Sal really liked my Mother, always wanting to be close to her, drinking her tea, and just generally being a pest. Wherever my Mother was, Sal was sure to be — sitting on her lap, drinking and eating whatever she was eating and drinking. Sal liked to put the handle of the spoon in his mouth and scoop the tea out of the cup with the bowl end, and then have a bite of what my mother was eating. After alternating the process for several minutes, he'd scoot very close to her ear. So we — Dave, my mother, and I — went to that yard with my mother's cup and a few crackers with peanut butter — and waited for Sal to come down from that tree. It wasn't a long wait.

The three of us must have made quite a sight, diligently coaxing a bird out of a tree. Eventually, Sal did come down. He probably needed to satisfy that caffeine fix — and seemed excited at the prospect of joining my mother for their afternoon tea. Catching Sal was easy this time — and off we went.

After a four-day excursion, Sal came back a very subdued bird. He would sit on his perch, gazing out the window making that soft clucking sound with his throat. Maybe he was dreaming about tall trees, freedom, and an unlimited supply of apples. Or perhaps Sal was planning new ways to irritate the dogs or devising a new plot to destroy the thermostat. Considering Sal was able to make a 'break' within the year, I suppose he was perfecting a new plan of escape.

SAL

Every so often, Sal visited All Creatures Animal Hospital in Urbana, Illinois. Dr. Ken Welle would give him a once-over and clip his nails, which felt like daggers when he landed on bare skin.

On this particular occasion, I arrived home and as I was getting out of my car, my neighbor Sam stopped to chat for a moment. I put Sal's cage on the ground next to the car, and in a flash, Sal managed to get the cage open and off he flew.

This was Sal's the third escape.

He immediately flew to the back of the house and found a spot in the tall pine tree. Sal was happy and began that relentless screaming, this time from delight. Soon, Sal had attracted a small audience. My young neighbor was really excited about the whole scene, but her mother quickly guided her into their house.

Dave had returned home by this time, so again, we were outside trying to convince a bird to come inside to either the delight or annoyance of the neighbors.

Darkness was fast approaching and Sal showed no signs of coming inside, no matter how much we coaxed.

Then I remembered that whenever the refrigerator opened, Sal came to investigate and maybe find a

"The Great Escapes"

The storm the day that Sal escaped...

treat. Perching on the open door, he would crane his neck to see what looked good, sometimes taking a small bite out of the insulation around the door, sometimes grabbing the butter and trying to fly off with it stuffed in his little beak. Usually I just gave the little darling a treat and shooed him away.

I began to open and shut the refrigerator a few times. Soon Sal flew closer and closer to the house. Eventually, curiosity and hunger won out and Sal flew inside, landing right on the refrigerator door.

Sal gave up his freedom once again, and this time was treated to some chocolate ice cream and an Oreo cookie.

There was one more quick escape before I investigated the idea of Sal's wings being clipped. Not as easy as it sounds.

"The Great Escapes"

Beautiful view from here

Even when bred in captivity, birds should not be considered domesticated animals. They are wild creatures whose natural instincts remain intact — and frustrated — when kept captive.

www.bornfreeusa.org

Once upon a midnight dreary,
while I pondered weak and weary,
Over many a quaint and curious volume of forgotten lore -
While I nodded, nearly napping,
suddenly there came a tapping,
As of some one gently rapping.

~ Edgar Allan Poem, "The Raven"

Sal and Mom, AKA Anna

Chapter 9

"My Mom and Sal"

Sal really liked my mom a.k.a. Anna Petrarca. He followed her, drank her tea, ate whatever she was eating, watched TV with her, looked at the paper she was reading — and in general, longed to be with her every possible second of every day. Much worse than having 20 three-year olds with the ability to fly and land on your shoulder. Frightening, isn't it?

Sal sipping tea and eating strawberries

When my mom tired of Sal's antics, she would go back to her room and shut the door expecting a little peace and quiet. Sal wouldn't stand for that. He waddled down the hall after her, stopping at her door, right under the door knob. He would occasionally crawl up the door frame and attempt to open the door — sometimes it worked, much to his delight and my mom's astonishment. She would shoo him away. But ever diligent, he began the process all over again, sometimes stopping and peeking under the door. Maybe to make sure she was there. Then with his beak, he would begin knocking on the door. At first it was funny — then we had to find ways to keep him away from the door. Finally, it was just work to keep him from being the single most bothersome creature on the earth. He never tired of this little exercise, because he never tired of wanting to be near my mom. Even when we moved and my mom lived upstairs, he found a way to the hall, hopped up the steps and knocked on her door. He never forgets and never gives up. There is something to say about his resolve and dedication. My mom might have characterized that a little differently.

Sal knocking on Anna's door!

My mother passed away in 2011, but even now, if you say the word 'grandma,' his little crown will go up and he looks around. We'll never know if Sal misses my mom, but I don't doubt that he remembers her. She is resting comfortably with the paper, a cup of tea, something sweet and no Sal. Truly heaven.

Many people mistakenly believe that all animals sold in pet shops are protected by laws. But while the federal Animal Welfare Act (AWA) mandates that certain animal facilities comply with licensing, inspection, and care requirements, retail pet stores (with the exception of those that sell "wild and exotic" animals) are not regulated under the Act. Furthermore, reptiles and parrots — the most commonly sold wild and exotic animals — are not currently covered under the provisions of the Act, leaving the majority of pet shops free from federal oversight.

www.bornfreeusa.org

SAL

Sal and Mom, AKA Anna

Although birds are unsuitable companion animals, their popularity as "pets" has exploded in the past few decades. An extensive 1998 demographic study estimated that there were 35-40 million birds kept as "pets" in the U.S — an increase of more than 250% from 1990

www.bornfreeusa.org

"My Mom and Sal"

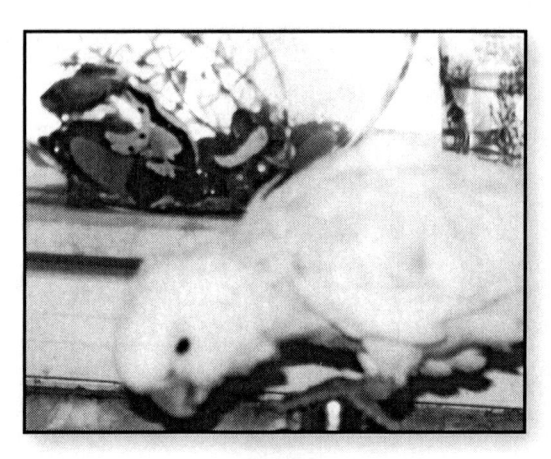

Bird Bath

The popularity of birds — whether captive-bred or wild-caught — as "pets" in the U.S. has enormous global influence, and fuels the trade in exotic birds around the world. The impact of the pet trade on wild parrot populations is devastating, with parrot species more globally threatened than almost any other major group of birds.

www.bornfreeusa.org

SAL

Sal sidling up to a picture of my mother

Use what talents you possess: the woods would be very silent if no birds sang there except those that sang best.

~ Henry Van Dyke

Don't cut my feathers!!!

Chapter 10

"Sal visits a clip joint"

Having had his escapes thwarted for the time being, Sal seemed to be on a new mission now, a mission that included destroying everything in and out of his path. Ceiling fans especially fascinated Sal. His personal merry-go-round gave him great delight. He had already

"Sal visits a clip joint"

dismantled one of the fans and was about to destroy the other one.

After chasing Sal away from my only remaining fan many times, I thought it was in his and my best interest to have Sal's wings clipped. Dave, Sal's non-feathered friend, advocated strongly that clipping the wings would be to deny Sal his "birdness." Maybe so, but I suggested we try it and see how much birdness was actually lost. I finally made the decision to visit Dr. Welle and get a few of Sal's feathers clipped. We returned home and for a

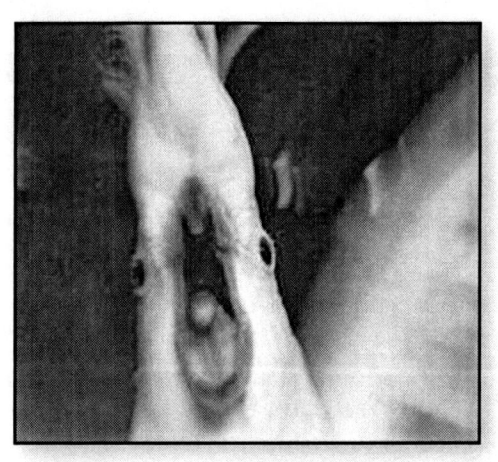

Sal expressing an opinion about the issue!

very short period of time, Sal walked everywhere, climbing up the furniture and curtains to get places. It wasn't long before Sal realized that he had strength we hadn't counted on — and again he made short flights around the house.

Thankfully the ceiling fans were out of reach. But now Sal spent more time on the floor and found new and exciting things to destroy, like rugs or shoes or whatever tickled his fancy. Oh, and the dog food was there. So Sal would perch on the dog dish for a little snack, much to the disgust of the dogs.

Life with Sal went along pretty uneventfully, until the fall of 2001, when Sal's "Christmas Miracle" occurred.

The stress of confinement can lead birds to a variety of abnormal behaviors, including excessive screaming, feather plucking, self-mutilation, and other destructive habits.

www.bornfreeusa.org

If the bird does like its cage, and does like its sugar, and will not leave it, why keep the door so very carefully shut?

~ Olive Schreiner

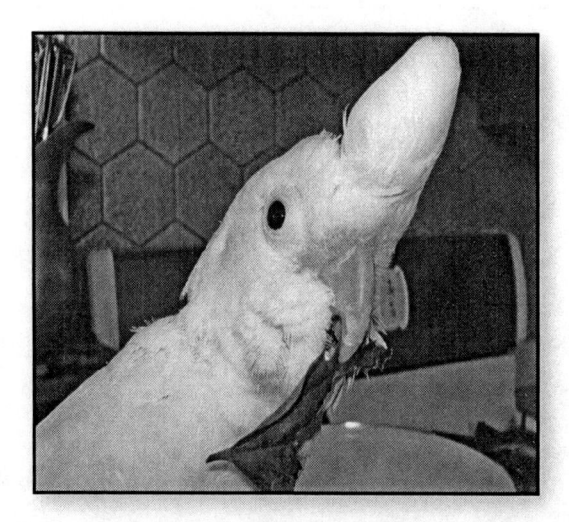

Wait till you hear this!

Chapter 11

"Sal's Christmas Miracle, 2001"

Sal and I spent a great deal of time together during the fall of 2001. I was recovering from knee replacement surgery and home more than usual. I was couchbound a great deal of the time, and Sal liked that.

"Sal's Christmas Miracle, 2001"

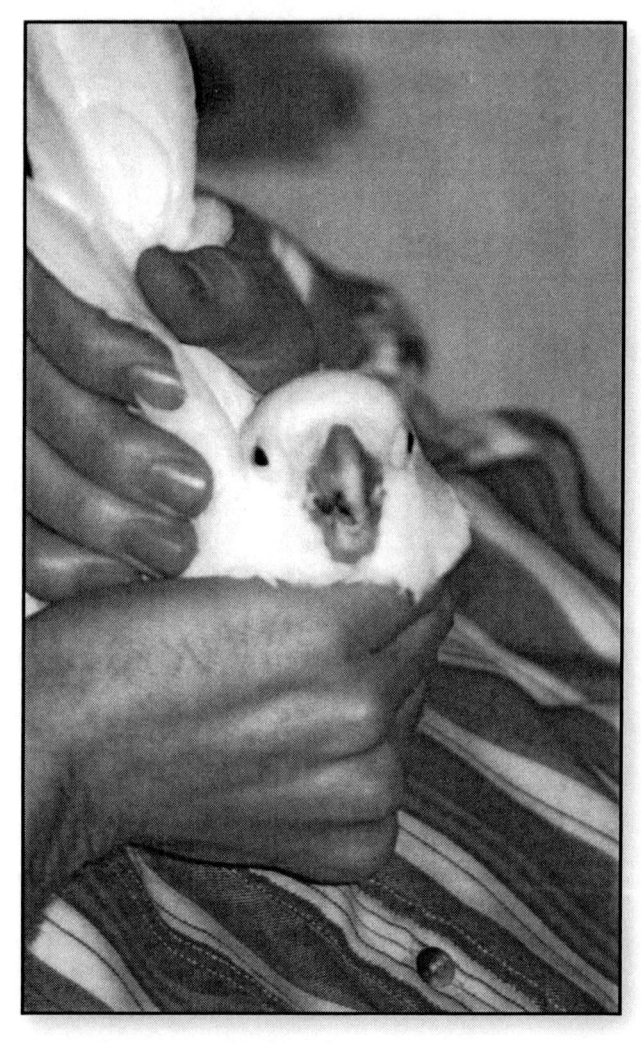

Sal and Dave

He wanted to be near me every second of every day. He constantly waddled over to where I was sitting on the couch, inspected my knee, and tilting his head to one side, made those weird clucking sounds. I spent our special time making sure Sal was nowhere near my knee. What a sight we were — me not able to move very well and Sal keeping watch over my knee — at least until the pain medicine kicked in, when Sal was banished to his room.

The surgery took place in early October of that year. By mid November, Sal was acting a bit stranger than usual, i.e., *very* strange. Sal had an old bread pan that he liked to burrow in, chewing up boxes or paper to make a soft little spot to slide into.

Sal was spending an unusual amount of time in that bread pan, thankfully more time in the pan than on me. Then Sal started regurgitating his food, trying hard to get that mess as close to me as possible.

The only activity that didn't change much had to do with Dave, Sal's non-feathered friend. Dave, holding Sal and stroking his back could coax the strangest sounds out of Sal. It was as though Sal were in a hypnotic state, making loud clucking noises and appearing to be disoriented, but happy.

This strange behavior escalated daily throughout November and December. At night, Sal would perch on a tree trunk that Dave brought home just for him. But that soon changed. Now in the

"Sal's Christmas Miracle, 2001"

morning when I got up, Sal was already in the bread pan doing his intense and seemingly important work. I was finally getting some peace, because Sal preferred the bread pan to me more and more. On the other hand, I thought there must be something wrong with the little guy. He was only interested in the bread pan, regurgitating — and getting that special attention from Dave every night.

I called Dr. Welle about a week before Christmas and made an appointment for Sal to be examined the next morning.

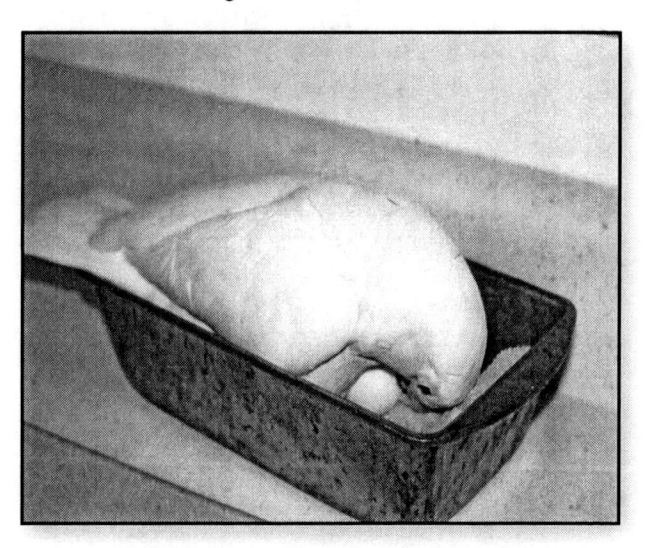

Sal and her Egg in the breadpan

I was up early the next day and so was Sal, already busy doing whatever it was that he was doing. Sal was in the bread pan clucking and shaking and completely oblivious to everything. I got Sal's carrier. Actually it was meant for a small dog — I had given up on the cage years before. When I attempted to take him out of the bread pan to put him in the carrier, he quickly escaped and went rushing back to the bread pan. So to save time, I placed Sal and the bread pan in the carrier and off we went to the doctor's office.

In the examining room, I pulled the bread pan out of the carrier, took a very wobbly and disoriented Sal out of the bread pan and looked down and saw

Sal's Egg

a little white object. I picked it up and said, "What is this?"

Dr. Welle said, "That would be an Egg."

At first I thought Dave had put a fake egg in the pan, but it was real. All these years we assumed Sal was male — but during that Christmas season, she decided to lay her first Egg.

Why, after all those years did he — I mean she — lay that Egg? There wasn't a male bird to fertilize the Egg — and what about the nest?

Dr. Welle said that perhaps Sal (or should we say Sally), apparently considered me or Dave (I think Dave) her mate, and the bread pan was his — I mean her nest. How special is that?

Well, the Egg was the hit of Christmas! When my family arrived, we spent lots of time looking at and talking about the Egg, the "Christmas Miracle of 2001." But all Sally wanted to do was lay on that Egg. That created a bit of a problem. Sally isn't the most sociable creature. When people are around, Sally goes to her room, so I had to devise little ways for Sally, the Egg, and my family to coexist without disrupting anyone. It all worked out — Sally had her Egg at various times throughout the day, and everyone had an Egg-cellent Christmas.

SAL

After a couple of weeks the Egg started to smell pretty bad. I planned on throwing it away when Sally wasn't looking, but eventually the Egg just disappeared. I never did find it and maybe it isn't

Daisy the Dove

necessary to know where it went. Only Sally knows for sure, and she isn't talking. Sally seemed to be lost for a while, but soon resumed her usual activities, like eating rugs or chewing through plaster while still maintaining her sweet personality.

Sal spent the next couple of years doing what she does best, annoying people and finding new and inventive ways to destroy stuff. Then came March of 2004, and Sally began to act rather weird again (weird for her has to be pretty weird). On March 24th, between 10 and 10:30 EST, Sally — while listening to Law and Order — laid Egg Number 2 in the hollowed out tree trunk that she loves to burrow in.

Sally had been acting strange for a few days, even by her standards. A few days before she laid the Egg, I took her to the vet in Pittsburgh to get her nails and wings clipped. We had a long long wait and during that time, it looked like she just might lay the Egg in the exam room. She was shaking and hunkering down in her carrier and when I took her out she shook even harder and appeared to be struggling. Might I finally witness the "Blessed" event? Not this time. The doctor came into the room and a very confused looking Sally abruptly stopped the process.

For the next few days, the regurgitation increased and Sally spent more time in the tree trunk, preparing for the Egg. Then about 9:30 the evening of the 24th, Sally retired to her room and out came Egg Number 2.

Then she laid an Egg during the presidential inauguration that was being broadcast on NPR.

Outside of Sally's window a dove, Daisy, was also preparing her nest, and soon there were little eggs soon to turn into little doves, because Daisy the Dove had Dan the Dove to fertilize her eggs.

So Sally and Daisy became friends, sort of.

Sally would scream and Daisy would look startled and fly away.

Ah, sweet mystery of life, someone said.

**A Robin Redbreast in a Cage
Puts all Heaven in a Rage.**

~ William Blake

Sal doing what she loves best, destroying something, this time a Kleenex box

Chapter 12

"The Miracle Continues"

Sally continues to lay her Eggs, usually during one of the many Law and Order shows. She sits on them for a few weeks and then seems to tire of this seemingly useless activity. I leave them for her, but a few have broken. Sort of sad. During the last several years Sally delivered several sets of

'Twins." One would usually break. Looking a bit confused, Sally would go back to taking care of the remaining Egg until that one would break. Then she begins to do what she does very well, annoy me.

Whether Sally is destined for something — good or bad, remains to be seen. She makes the best of what she has, sometimes causing problems for those around her — me for instance — but always finds something to fill her days. She still looks

Sally's Twins

longingly outside, where she should be. Sally will be around for a while longer doing what she does best, whatever that is.

Until then…it's a laugh a minute!

Sal raiding a purse for chewing gum

We think caged birds sing, when indeed they cry.

~ John Webster

Proper Nutrition for Pet Birds

Information about Proper Nutrition and General Care for birds is provided by All Creatures Animal Hospital in Urbana, Illinois
www.allcreaturesah.com

Seed Based Diets

- Birds will select what looks best, not what is good for them.
- Seed diets are deficient in 20-25 nutrients.
- Vegetables and fruits are 85-95% water.
- Seeds are very high in calories.
- Nearly all birds on this type of diet exhibit signs of malnutrition!

Aren't Seeds the Natural Diet?

- Only superficially.
- Seeds are only available at certain seasons.

- Parent birds normally teach good eating habits.
- Wild and domestic seed crops are different.
- Wild birds work hard for a living and need extra calories.

What About the Vitamins I Give?

- Vitamin supplements are a poor way to improve the diet.
- They lose potency in water and are not consumed if sprinkled on dry seed.
- Supplements promote bacterial growth in the water.
- Most have very inaccurate means of dosing.

Table Foods

- Table foods vary in value to your bird.
- Many are so high in water that they amount to a very small part of the diet.
- Some are potentially dangerous.
- One potato chip is analogous to a whole bag for a human.

My Bird Won't Eat That!

- Birds eat what they are accustomed to.
- Texture and appearance are the most important factors in food selection.
- Birds must be trained to eat proper foods.
- Too many choices allow the bird to choose only the familiar food.
- Virtually any bird can be converted to a good diet.

Is It Worth Changing the Diet?

- Yes!
- Pet birds live 20 to 60 years or more. A diet change now can have a big impact.
- Birds are livelier and more vibrant when on a healthy diet.

Ideal Diets

- Formulated diets should be 50-75% of diet.
- Remainder of diet should be 50% grains and 50% vegetables.
- Emphasize greens, yellow and orange vegetables, and legumes.

- Supplements should not be given.
- Grit is unnecessary for pet birds.

Formulated Diets

- Formulated diets have all known required nutrients compressed into each nugget.
- While not perfect, these represent the best way to assure proper nutrition.
- Many brands are available to choose from.
- Supplements are unnecessary and potentially dangerous to birds on formulated diets.

Converting the Diet

- Seeds must be limited to a little less than what is normally consumed.
- The seed is mixed with the new diet so the bird must dig through the new food.
- The seed is then gradually reduced and then eliminated from the diet.
- If your bird looks bad, go back to seeds and start all over.

Conversion Tips

- Use a soft diet (rice/bean/vegetable mix) to hold seed and pellets together.
- Feed in familiar dishes.
- Let your bird see another bird eating the new food.
- Pretend to eat the food yourself.
- Try again if first time doesn't work.
- Try feeding one meal with pellets in the morning and a meal with seeds in the evening.

Nail Trimming

- Why?
- Client comfort
- Patient safety
- mproved pet/owner bond

Wing Trimming

- Why?
- Prevent escape
- Prevent injuries
- Improve behavior

Band Removal

- Why?
- Some risk of catching on things, leading to injury
- Doesn't fit
- Accumulation of keratin/debris under band

Preventative Health Care

- Early recognition and treatment of medical problems
- Development of a medical baseline
- Vaccination against infectious diseases
- Client education
- Establish a client/patient/doctor relationship

Physical Exams

- Upon acquisition of the bird
- 3 months later
- 6 months after second exam
- 9 months after the third
- Annually thereafter
- Can reveal a lot of information about the general status of the bird.

- Subtle problems can be missed with a physical examination alone.

Laboratory Evaluation

- Birds are good at "masking" signs of illness.
- Laboratory analysis can detect subclinical diseases.
- Some tests should be done each visit; others just initially.
- Some depend on the species, age, source, and purpose of the bird.

Vaccines

- Polyomavirus and Pacheco's disease are the only available vaccines for pet parrots at this time.
- Birds at risk should be vaccinated at 5 and 7 weeks and then annually.
- Some birds develop vaccine site granulomas.
- Discuss this with one of us if you are interested.

Establish Veterinary Caregiver

- The best time to develop a relationship with an avian veterinarian is not during an emergency.
- Ask about our hours, policies, and emergency procedures.
- Find out if you're comfortable with our style of practice.

An Ounce of Prevention

- Early recognition allows more successful treatment of problems.
- Recognizing serious health problems allows new birds to be returned to the seller.
- Preventative medicine is less costly than emergency medicine.

SAL

Birds eat a lot, some say at least half their weight in food every day. So, if you are 120 pounds, you would be eating about 60 pounds of food. Sal eats all day — bird food, my food, lots of pasta, fruits and vegetables, plants — and anything else she can sink her beak into, until I put her to bed. And some young birds eat more than their weight in food every day.

Special thanks to Joyce Faulkner, Dave Gire, Lori Walker, and Pat Kaley.

Much love to my favorite Aunt Elsie — and to Ginny too.

ANNA MARIE PETRARCA GIRE publishes Women's Yellow Pages, a yearly print and digital magazine in Southwest Pennsylvania. She also publishes an on line news magazine that is sent to subscribers nationally and internationally. Ms Gire provided legal advocacy to survivors of sexual and domestic violence in Illinois and volunteered at domestic and sexual violence centers in Pittsburgh, Pennsylvania.

Ms Gires' only connection to birds, prior to Sal, was looking at them, feeding them and listening to their many beautiful songs in the spring. Ms Gire resides in Pittsburgh, Pennsylvania — and shares her space with Sal.

CPSIA information can be obtained at www.ICGtesting.com
Printed in the USA
BVOW03s0812270913

332201BV00009B/211/P

9 781937 958183